Growth and Change

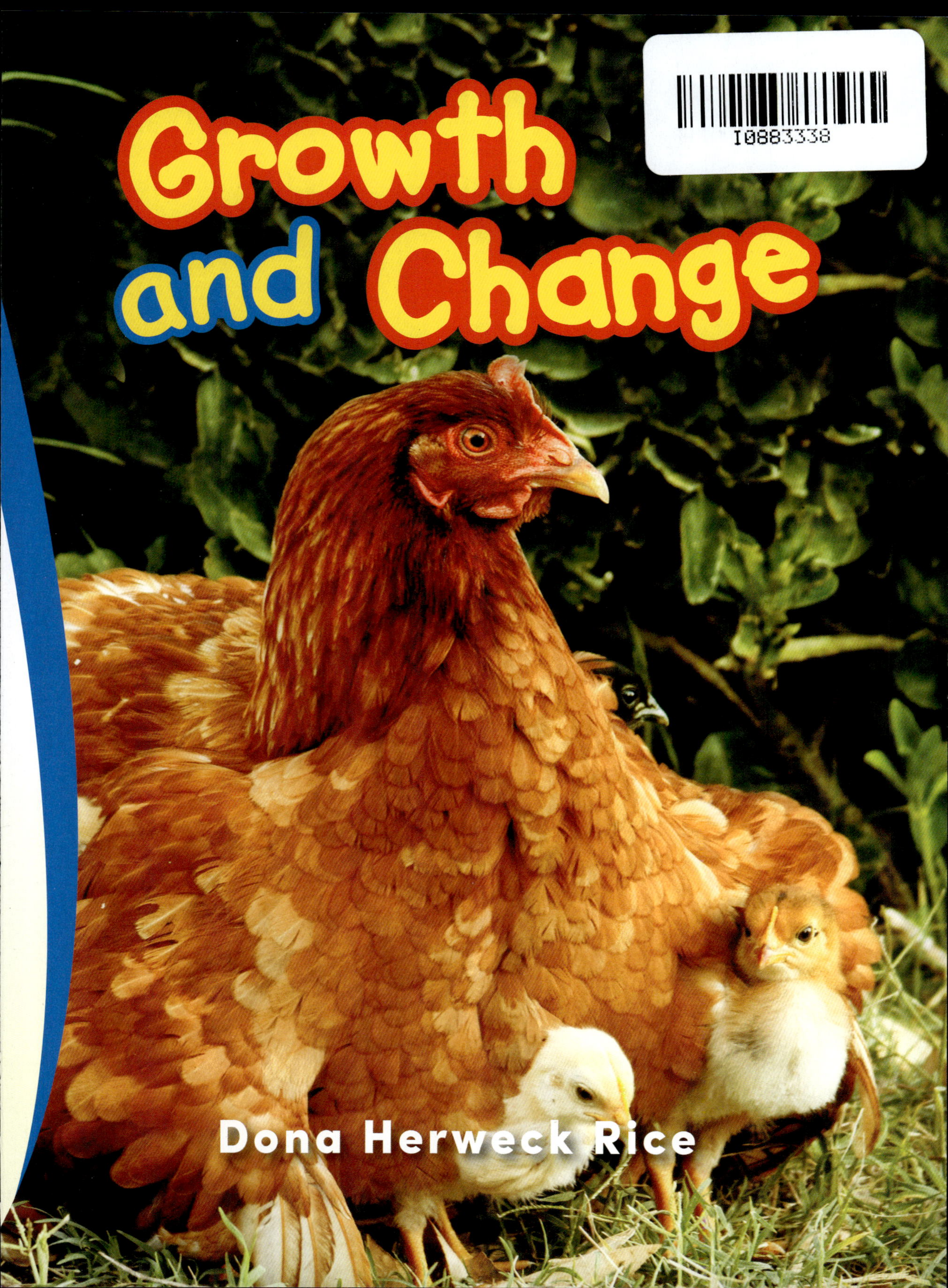

Dona Herweck Rice

Consultants

Sally Creel, Ed.D.
Curriculum Consultant

Leann Iacuone, M.A.T., NBCT, ATC
Riverside Unified School District

Jill Tobin
California Teacher of the Year
Semi-Finalist
Burbank Unified School District

Image Credits: p.17 (bottom) Blaine Harrington III/Alamy; p.15 (bottom) FLPA/Alamy; p.15 (top) National Geographic Image Collection/Alamy; p.9 (top) Hiroya Minakuchi/Getty Images; pp.20–21 (illustrations) Janelle Bell-Martin; all other images from Shutterstock.

Library of Congress Cataloging-in-Publication Data

Rice, Dona, author.
Growth and change / Dona Herweck Rice; consultants, Sally Creel, Ed.D. curriculum consultant, Leann Iacuone, M.A.T., NBCT, ATC Riverside Unified School District, Jill Tobin, California Teacher of the Year Semi-Finalist Burbank Unified School District.
pages cm
Includes index.
ISBN 978-1-4807-4562-9 (pbk.)
ISBN 978-1-4807-5052-4 (ebook)
1. Growth—Juvenile literature.
2. Developmental biology—Juvenile literature. I. Title.
QP84.R475 2015
571.8—dc23

2014013146

Teacher Created Materials
5301 Oceanus Drive
Huntington Beach, CA 92649-1030
http://www.tcmpub.com

ISBN 978-1-4807-4562-9

Printed by: 51497
Printed in: China

Table of Contents

Little Ones

Each animal begins as a baby.

There are many kinds of babies.

Some babies **hatch** from eggs.

Penguins hatch from eggs.

Some babies grow inside their mothers.

Kittens grow inside their mothers.

Growing Up

Every baby grows up.

Baby elephants get very big.

They start small. Then, they get bigger. Some get huge!

The Biggest

The biggest animal in the world is the blue whale. An adult can be as big as three school buses!

Some babies are born **bald**.

Naked mole rats will never grow hair or fur.

They may grow hair or **fur** later. Some may not.

Fur

Fur is like hair. But it is thicker.

Pandas grow fur as they get older.

Some babies are born with lots of hair.

Then, they just grow hairier!

Others never have hair.

A baby frog is born as a tadpole.

They have **scales** or bare skin.

Snakes, lizards, and fish have scales.

Scales

Scales are thin plates that protect an animal's skin.

No matter how it is born, each baby needs the same **basic** (BEY-sik) things.

This calf eats grass.

A baby needs water and food. It needs to **breathe**, too.

This fish breathes under water.

This lion cub drinks water.

And a baby needs to play and get plenty of rest. Just like you!

These kittens play with their mother.

This lamb rests
with its mother.

Let's Do Science!

What do animals near you need to live? Try this and see!

What to Get

- magnifying glass
- paper and pencil
- plastic gloves

What to Do

1. Put on your gloves. Go outside with an adult.

2. Look for signs of animal life. Pick things up and study them. (But do not pick up animals!)

3. What do you see and hear? Do you see things that animals eat? Do you see where they live?

4. Make a chart like this one. Write what you observe. Then, write what that tells you about the animals.

What I observe	What this tells me about animals

Glossary

bald—having no fur or hair

basic—main or most important part

breathe—to take in and let out air or water

fur—the soft, thick coat of an animal

hatch—born by coming out of an egg

scales—small, thin plates that protect the skin of some animals

Index

Your Turn!

Watch an Animal

Find an animal. It may be your pet. It may be an animal you see outside. Watch it carefully. (Be sure you are safe.) What can you tell about its needs? Draw a picture of what you see.